Wisdom of Nature

Leadership Lessons for All of Us

Jenna Forster

Copyright © Jenna Forster, 2016.

All rights reserved. No part of this publication may be reproduced, distributed, or transmitted in any form or by any means, including photocopying, recording, or other electronic or mechanical methods, without the prior written permission of the publisher, except in the case of brief quotations embodied in critical reviews and certain other noncommercial uses permitted by copyright law.

Paperback Edition

ISBN-10: 1539181227
ISBN-13: 978-1539181224

Disclaimer:

Although the author and publisher have made every effort to ensure that the information in this book was correct at press time, the author and publisher do not assume and hereby disclaim any liability to any party for any loss, damage, or disruption caused by errors or omissions, whether such errors or omissions result from negligence, accident, or any other cause.

Published by:
JF and Associates
www.JFandAssociates.com

Edited & Prepared for Publication by:
Jennifer-Crystal Johnson
www.JenniferCrystalJohnson.com

Dedication

To all the current and future leaders in our world. Life, like leadership, does not have to be complicated. On the contrary! When you know what you are looking for, both life and leadership become very simple. My hope for this book is to inspire you to simplify your approach, streamline your communication, and work together to achieve the greatness you have always wanted.

Wisdom of Nature | Jenna Forster

Contents

Acknowledgments	7
Introduction	9
Perseverance	11
Trust & Partnership	15
Independence vs. Interdependence	19
Leading with Ease	23
Understanding Opportunities	27
Strength to the Core	31
Parting Words	35
About the Author	36

Acknowledgments

I would like to acknowledge the talented individuals who supplied the artistic components of this book. Its incredible photographs were supplied by the inspiring Danielle Weir, Kristopher Clausen, and Lynn Mathieson. I would also like to thank the wonderful Geri Sera for her continued support and contribution to my life, my work, my inspiration, and this book. These individuals represent our future leaders, our youth, and our current leaders. Thank you to all of you for your contributions!

Introduction

Leadership. Quite a word, don't you think? I have had the pleasure of spending a great deal of time, money, and energy researching, reading, and discussing the topic of leadership. Leadership is a word – only a word – but one that tends to bring up some sort of emotion in most of us. I've heard things like, "Leadership has been marketed to death," "Leadership is a dictatorship," "Leadership has a style," "Leadership is a farce," "Leadership is inspiring," and the list goes on. But what *is* leadership?

I've come to believe that leadership is reflected in our relationships with others, the causes we choose to take on, and the direction we choose to follow. Finding leadership examples doesn't have to be complex. To explore what I mean, let's examine simple and inspiring forms of leadership through the beauty and clarity of the governance found in nature. Spending time in nature and really observing the beautiful dance around us will bring wisdom and, perhaps, more appreciation to this sometimes elusive characteristic – leadership.

Core values within a well-rounded leadership style differ from one leader to another, but here are a few of the values I've found to be key in my leadership portfolio.

What does leadership mean to you?

Perseverance

Where can I resource the inspiration I require to be more sustained and to persevere when life's challenges seem overwhelming?

If perseverance is a component of leadership, how am I evidencing it in my leadership style?

_____

_____

_____

_____

_____

_____

Leadership, like life, may feel overwhelming and all-consuming at different times for each of us. I do not believe the solution always lies in putting our head down and pushing through. The old adage, "You have to work hard to be successful," is not necessarily accurate in most challenges. Our solutions most likely lie in working smarter, not harder. I propose that, as seen in this flower, the power of perseverance comes from recognizing where the spaces of opportunities lie. Slowing down to recognize the opportunities of breakthrough and growth will allow us to push forward with confidence and true understanding.

Perseverance is a core trait of strong leaders; the ability to press forward despite insurmountable obstacles. This trait can be seen over and over again in both past and current leaders. As we move through life, we enter into our own journey; one with love, loss, success, laughter, challenges, and so on. Many times it seems easier to throw in the towel and hide away or disconnect from those around us. It is natural to recede and pull away when times get tough. While this may feel safe initially, disconnection stemming from fear rarely has positive outcomes. As our leadership capacity grows in our family, our business, and our relationships, we will find that disconnecting is detrimental to our progress.

We may feel we are alone, surrounded by a severe or barren environment. A typical barren and harsh landscape may be mountainous or very rocky, lack soil or only offer sand for sustenance, and usually has limited access to water. But, throughout the terrain, we will find plant growth, weeds, bushes, and even strong and inspiring trees. How can such growth take place? What makes a plant so powerful that it can grow over rock and survive in sand with very little nourishment? What creates that strong, steady perseverance that allows for such growth? Is it that the plant's fundamental purpose is so strong it will bring to every capacity all the necessary resources to fulfil the measure of its creation?

Such striking views in nature have taught me that leadership is not just about having a grand vision or about being visible to others. More importantly, it is about understanding why I do what I do to such a degree that I evidence my values in my actions to the point of influencing events and other people without even realizing any effect is taking place. Just as this plant grows for the sake of growing, true influence without ego comes with a sense of ease and our focus remains balanced on all parties at hand. Energy and effort becomes about creation. As we merge and fuse core values in our relationships and strive to positively enhance one another's lives, our communities and our world will be advanced. Our leadership will become very visible to both ourselves and those around us. We will move away from the need or fear that surrounds us and toward the strong, solid ability that is already inside every one of us.

Remember a time when you persevered through obstacles and circumstances to come out stronger on the other side.

Wisdom of Nature | Jenna Forster

Wisdom of Nature | Jenna Forster

Trust & Partnership

Are there examples found in nature I can connect to of relationships or partnerships based on trust?

Do I spread my wings to keep my partners sustained and secure?

Leadership is not readily apparent in a void or space without other people.

This was brought to my awareness while I sat at the beach watching a floating log hosting a grouping of birds all perched in a single line atop it. As the wave motion on the water caused the log to bob about, I watched one and sometimes two of the birds as they intermittently spread their wings wide. At first I wasn't sure what they were doing, but then I realized that every time there were gusts of wind, the birds repeated the action of spreading their wings. As the birds spread their wings, they kept the log steady and supported all the other birds perching on the log. There was a level of trust and partnership felt within the birds to create safety and success for each of them.

In influential leadership relationships there is trust and partnership. We have a deep understanding that everyone and everything in our lives are connected in some way. Simply sustaining one another by taking appropriate action in teams builds trust to sustain the relationships and the partners. It strengthens the partnerships. Leaders find a way to steady circumstances when the wind inevitably blows. While we may not be able to see the outcome or have discomfort in our feelings toward the unknown, we also have a foundational understanding of the resources that surround us and the strengths we and everyone around us bring to the table. Sometimes leaders actually become the, "wind beneath our wings," lifting us to capacities we would never discover without their support.

Leadership involves the awareness, understanding, and capacity to steady and build those around us to such a degree that they begin to do the same. When we as leaders move our focus from, "What can I do for me?" and to the direction of, "What can I do for those around me?" the beautiful dance of strength and poise is accomplished. The next time you find yourself at a loss, stop and ask yourself, "How may I serve?" As you focus on contribution to the whole instead of each individual component, you will start to see how the puzzle of what is necessary begins to unfold. Remember, those around you are a direct reflection of you. Make sure that reflection is what you want to see when you look in the mirror.

What are five habits you can implement every day to serve others and contribute to the whole as a leader?

_____

_____

_____

_____

_____

_____

Wisdom of Nature | Jenna Forster

Wisdom of Nature | Jenna Forster

Independence vs. Interdependence

Where am I connected with others?

How does my interconnectivity impact the course of action in my life and positively influence the lives of others daily?

_____

_____

_____

_____

_____

_____

_____

I live in a beautiful part of the world surrounded by endless green and mountainous landscapes edged by the Pacific Ocean. The breath of the sea is like the breath of life to me. My world is somewhat predictable and reliable, yet when life's events unexpectedly tip too far in one direction or another, I have lost my balance. I have even felt I may be in danger.

I've come to know that if we don't care for our bodies, our minds, and our spirits, we cannot assume to call upon our full capacities. It is the same if we do not care for our local environment, our oceans, or our planet. We can see how our global weather or climate is impacted. Even the predictability and reliability of the seasons are altered as we neglect the intricate balance of nature and fail to care for all components involved.

There will be moments when leaders are both independent and interdependent – like our seas. As I look out at what seems to be a solo rock sticking out of the water, I can feel its strength and independence. But what I also know is that, surrounding that seemingly solo rock, is a multitude of sea life: barnacles, crustaceans, eels, crabs, seaweed, and micro-organisms that all co-exist for the sake of their benefit and survival. The interdependence taking place below the water's surface allows each to thrive, and while we may not be able to see below the surface, it is important to understand it is there.

As leaders, we are not solo monarchs – or, if we are, our leadership will have a date stamp on it. We are each partnered with other people and circumstances influencing everything around us. When we see ourselves as part of everything instead of independent from or above things, we will begin to look at the ripple effect we have every moment of every day on everyone with whom we engage. As human beings, we have a mirror effect happening underneath the surface of relationships. Unless we are consciously aware, we are either mirroring the behaviour we see or another is mirroring ours. When we have appreciation beyond ourselves, we can better participate in the symphony of our interdependence.

Name five things you appreciate about the people around you; those you lead, work with, go to school with, or live with.

Wisdom of Nature | Jenna Forster

Wisdom of Nature | Jenna Forster

Leading with Ease

Do I need to struggle to lead?

Does my leadership come with ease and flexibility or is it choppy, controlling others with a tightened noose?

As I lay in the tall grass, watching it sway back and forth with the grace and ease orchestrated by the shifting breezes, I felt peace and delight. The grass, having such an understanding of the environment around it and its role in that environment, has no fear of being moved by something outside of itself. As the wind shifts and momentarily disappears, the grass once again comes back to its center and stands tall. The awareness was beautiful and revealing.

A great deal of our time may be spent fighting to control situations, individuals, or circumstances. I consistently examine my leadership to determine if I feel the need to control or manipulate rather than to move in concert with and positively influence others. I strive to overcome the tendency to be focused on leading those around me while forgetting that leadership starts with me. All of us have the capacity to move in a forward direction with ease and grace once we understand we should let go of the fight. A disconnection within us may cause us to force others, requiring them to align with us… like our way is the only "right" way!

I believe this fight is based on fear. When I try to control a situation, individual, or team, I must realize something is wrong and I'm functioning from a fearful state. A need for control reflects our fears about losing control, doing it wrong, self-doubt, and even personal insecurity. When I feel the need to tighten my grip, to control, I ask myself, "What am I afraid of?" I'm learning to strive for flexibility and vision. I want to move forward with a greater sense of trust, grace, and ease; one that doesn't come with the physical sensation of constriction. As leaders, the act of stepping back and taking an umbrella view of what is really going on and reconnecting to what it is we are trying to accomplish can allow us to let go of control, intensity, and tension and move forward with deliberation and ease.

Is fear getting in your way? Be honest with yourself. What are you afraid of?

Wisdom of Nature | Jenna Forster

Understanding Opportunities

What are the opportunities around me?

Who or what naturally contributes to outcomes I seek in my life?

While standing by the river's edge, it is impossible to miss the continuous flow of the water as it swirls around boulders, darts into cracks, and sweeps over rocks. Nature creates sites for continuous momentum. In our lives, we must understand momentum; unexpected flows in our daily challenges and experiences are circumstances for choices. Water seldom works against where gravity influences it to go. It finds gaps and moves forward or, when in an unnatural housing like a dam, it may escape and cause great destruction en route to its final destination.

I've spent time as a leader straining against obstacles and pushing boulders uphill. I wasn't looking for the opening, the need, the gap to be filled, or to serve the greater good as I have made choices to act. Rivers have a purpose, a direction, a course. Leadership requires the same efficiency and effective awareness of direction, purpose, and course. As a leader, I must make choices for influence and action in alignment with the purpose, direction, and course needed to attain desired outcomes.

I'm learning to use a portion of my time to look at the opportunities ahead of me to determine how my team and I will comfortably make choices contributing to each opportunity. When I'm in life's river, I want to dance amid obstacles, making choices that fill needs allowed by obvious openings. When ease takes over and I effortlessly flow through and around my obstacles, I will sense I am doing the right thing, making the right choice, communicating the right words. This internal intelligence always knows the answer and we can trust it.

Name a time when making decisions felt effortless to you. Remember that feeling vividly; this is when you're in the flow of life. Your purpose and direction are perfectly aligned with what you must do. How did things turn out?

Wisdom of Nature | Jenna Forster

Wisdom of Nature | Jenna Forster

Strength to the Core

What makes us able to stand strong and steady through all forces of opposition?

What strength can be found in our roots and how deep are they?

A willow tree, growing strong and solid, has many roles in nature's process. Its roots are deep and far-stretching, allowing the tree to withstand all types of adversity. The tree may lose a few branches along the way, but at its core, its stature and strength are unwavering. A tree has many roles in our natural world such as providing shelter, cleaning our air, and beautifying our environment. Leaders also play many roles in their environment, roles that require a stature of unwavering strength and responsibility.

In order to withstand the winds that will blow, leaders understand and embrace the core needs or values involved in their leadership. Those core needs that make or break our style of leadership may be feelings, wants, passions, or cares that keep us strong and steadily growing stronger and upward. When we are not aware of our roots – what we stand for and care about, our values – it is very difficult to maintain our strength, to understand our responsibility, and to be accountable when that time comes.

Taking some time to really think about, listen, and become aware of our values can ground and teach us to withstand future forces or weather that may come our way. When we dismiss this information, we will find ourselves weakened and vulnerable to the forces of nature in our environment. We will find ourselves taking action for the sake of pleasing others, to avoid disappointment, or perhaps to prove our worth to someone or something. Our actions become someone else's and our foundation cracks. I am constantly checking in to be sure growth in my life is based on what I want, as that is the only way to keep the strong, sturdy growth true to me.

Take a few minutes to write down five of your core values. What are they? How strongly do you feel about them? What has happened in the past when you allowed those values to be compromised?

Wisdom of Nature | Jenna Forster

Parting Words

Traits such as Perseverance, Trust & Partnership, Independence vs. Interdependence, Leading with Ease, Understanding Opportunities, and Strength to the Core have been pivotal to my success as a leader. As you move through the rough waters, the calm seas, and the beautiful sunrises, may your leadership and impact be filled with a sense of inner peace, confidence, and grounding. We all have a tremendous ability inside of us, a purity that, like symbols of nature, are prominent in our being. With a little awareness, information, understanding, and knowledge, that ability will come forth and we will then move through life step by step with an internal intelligence that is as powerful as nature itself. I believe we, as human beings, are driven to make a contribution during the course of our lives. I hope this book has allowed for some thoughts to percolate, which is the start of everything. I close with a quote I live by:

"A good head and a good heart are always a formidable combination." – Nelson Mandela

Go forward with a good head and a good heart; make your contribution to this world of ours and may your life be filled with joy, love, happiness, and understanding.

To your continued success!

Jenna Forster

About the Author

Jenna Forster is an Executive Coach, Neuroscience Specialist, and Leadership Development Expert. Her life's work is to integrate Neuroscience and Coaching to serve her clients at the highest level.

Coach, Teacher, Author
jf@jfandassociates.com

www.ingramcontent.com/pod-product-compliance
Lightning Source LLC
Chambersburg PA
CBHW070424190526
45169CB00003B/1394